JR. GRAPHIC MONSTER STORIES

WITCHES!

MARK CHEATHAM

PowerKiDS press.

New York

Published in 2012 by The Rosen Publishing Group, Inc.

29 East 21st Street, New York, NY 10010

First Edition

Editor: Joanne Randolph

Book Design: Planman Technologies

Illustrations: Planman Technologies

Library of Congress Cataloging-in-Publication Data

Cheatham, Mark.

Witches! / by Mark Cheatham. — 1st ed.

   p. cm. — (Jr. graphic monster stories)

Includes index.

ISBN 978-1-4488-6224-5 (library binding) — ISBN 978-1-4488-6407-2 (pbk.) — ISBN 978-1-4488-6408-9 (6-pack)

1. Witches—United States—History—18th century—Comic books, strips, etc. —Juvenile literature. I. Title.

BF1573.C54 2012

133.4'3—dc23

2011027914

Manufactured in the United States of America

CPSIA Compliance Information: Batch #PLW2102PK: For Further Information contact Rosen Publishing, New York, New York at 1-800-237-9932

Contents

Main Characters

Grace Sherwood (1660–1740) **Accused** in court of being a witch, Sherwood tried to prove her **innocence**. Known as the Witch of Pungo, she is the subject of many stories and tales.

John and Jane Gisburne (c. 1700s) In 1698, accused Grace Sherwood of killing their cotton crop and pigs with witchcraft. Sherwood successfully **sued** them for making false statements.

Elizabeth Barnes (c. 1700s) Accused Grace Sherwood of acts of witchcraft. Sherwood successfully sued her for making false statements.

Elizabeth Hill (c. 1700s) In 1705, she was successfully sued by Grace Sherwood for assault. Hill accused Sherwood of witchcraft leading to her court trial the following year.

Witch Facts

- In Colonial America, people believed that witches made **pacts** with the Devil. The Devil would leave a "Devil's mark" on the body of the witch. The body of an accused witch was searched for the mark. Birthmarks or moles were often used to **convict** a person of witchcraft.

- During Colonial times, it was commonly believed that a witch could turn herself into a bird or other animal. To make this change, the witch would rub herself with an ointment called witch butter, a grease made from graveyard bodies.

- It was thought that witches especially liked to change into black cats. That is why it was bad luck to kill a cat.

Witches!

"MANY THOUGHT THE CHILDREN WERE UNDER THE SPELLS OF WITCHES. EVENTUALLY, MORE THAN 200 PEOPLE WERE ACCUSED OF BEING WITCHES. SALEM HELD MANY WITCH TRIALS."

"MANY OF THE SO-CALLED WITCHES WERE SENTENCED TO DEATH BY HANGING."

THANKS, LISA. GOOD WORK. DO ANY OF YOU KNOW WHAT WAS AT THE ROOT OF THE SALEM WITCH TRIALS? WELL, I WILL EXPLAIN.

SALEM WITCH MUSEUM

"THE PORTER AND PUTNAM FAMILIES COMPETED FOR POWER IN THE SALEM CHURCH. THE PUTNAMS SUPPORTED THE REVEREND PARRIS, AND THE PORTERS DID NOT. THE PUTNAMS TOOK THE LEAD IN ACCUSING PEOPLE OF WITCHCRAFT.

"'THE PARRISES' DAUGHTER WAS AN ACCUSER. SOON ALL OF SALEM LIVED IN FEAR OF BEING A **VICTIM** OF WITCHCRAFT OR OF BEING ACCUSED OF BEING A WITCH."

"AFTER SOME TIME, MANY PEOPLE STARTED TO BELIEVE THAT THE ACCUSATIONS WERE LIES. BY MAY 1763, THE MASSACHUSETTS GOVERNOR **PARDONED** ALL OF THOSE IN PRISON WHO WERE ACCUSED OF WITCHCRAFT."

"IN THE LATE 1600S, GRACE SHERWOOD LIVED ON A FARM WITH HER HUSBAND AND SONS IN PUNGO, VIRGINIA, NEAR VIRGINIA BEACH.

"SHERWOOD WAS DIFFERENT FROM OTHER WOMEN. SHE SPOKE HER MIND. SHE WORE MEN'S CLOTHING. SHE GREW HERBS AND WORKED AS A HEALER. NEIGHBORS BECAME SUSPICIOUS OF HER."

GRACE IS VERY STRANGE.

THOSE HERBS CAN BE USED TO MAKE WITCH'S TEA, YOU KNOW.

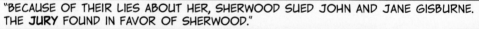

"THE SAME YEAR, ELIZABETH BARNES ALSO TOLD STORIES ABOUT SHERWOOD."

TELL THEM WHAT HAPPENED, ELIZABETH!

"A FEW DAYS EARLIER, BARNES SAID SHE AWOKE TO FIND GRACE SHERWOOD NEXT TO HER BED."

SHE WASN'T ALONE. I SAW HER WITH THE DEVIL!

"WHEN BARNES GOT UP, THE DEVIL VANISHED. SHERWOOD GREW FANGS AND CLAWS AND LEAPT ONTO BARNES'S BACK!"

"SHERWOOD THEN TURNED INTO A BLACK CAT AND ESCAPED THROUGH THE KEYHOLE!"

"GRACE SHERWOOD AND HER HUSBAND SUED ELIZABETH BARNES FOR THE LIES SHE TOLD. AGAIN, SHE WON IN COURT."

"IN 1705, ELIZABETH HILL, A NEIGHBOR, **ATTACKED** GRACE SHERWOOD."

"SHERWOOD TOOK ELIZABETH HILL TO COURT. SHE WAS FOUND GUILTY OF ATTACKING GRACE SHERWOOD."

"A MONTH AFTER THE TRIAL, THE COURT CHARGED SHERWOOD WITH WITCHCRAFT."

YOU WILL SEARCH GRACE SHERWOOD'S BODY FOR WITCH'S MARKS THAT COULD HAVE BEEN LEFT BY THE DEVIL.

HER BODY HAS STRANGE MARKS WE HAVE NEVER BEFORE SEEN!

NONSENSE! I AM NO WITCH!

"THE **MAGISTRATES** ORDERED THE SHERIFF TO ARREST GRACE SHERWOOD.

"THE COURT PROPOSED A DUCKING FOR SHERWOOD. THIS MEANT SHE WOULD BE BOUND AND THROWN IN THE WATER TO PROVE HER GUILT OR INNOCENCE."

"A LARGE CROWD CAME TO WATCH THE DUCKING. SHERWOOD'S HANDS WERE BOUND TO HER FEET. THE SHERIFF ROWED HER TO DEEP WATER."

"SHERWOOD BROKE FREE FROM THE ROPES AND MADE HER WAY TO SHORE."

WITCH!

"PEOPLE SAID THAT SHERWOOD **PREDICTED** THAT ALL WHO WATCHED HER DUCKING WOULD ALSO GET WET. A VIOLENT STORM BLEW ASHORE.

"AFTER SERVING A FEW MONTHS IN JAIL, SHERWOOD WAS RELEASED. AT LAST, HER NEIGHBORS LEFT HER ALONE TO LIVE A QUIET LIFE."

"HOWEVER, THE LEGEND OF THE WITCH OF PUNGO GREW. IT WAS SAID THAT WHEN SHE WAS RELEASED FROM JAIL, SHE ASKED FOR TWO DIRTY PLATES."

DON'T BE SILLY! HA HA HA!

THESE PLATES WILL HELP ME FLY HOME.

"SHERWOOD ROSE INTO THE SKY USING THE PLATES LIKE WINGS."

HA HA HA HA!

"PEOPLE SAY THAT ONE DAY SHERWOOD NEEDED ROSEMARY, AN HERB, FOR A DISH SHE WAS COOKING. SHE NEEDED TO GET ROSEMARY FROM EUROPE."

I NEED SOME HERBS FOR THIS DISH!

"SHE TOOK A SHIP IN THE HARBOR AND SAILED IT TO EUROPE THAT NIGHT.

"BY MORNING SHE RETURNED WITH HER ROSEMARY. SHE SAILED BACK TO VIRGINIA IN AN EGGSHELL!

"PEOPLE SAID THAT WHEN SHERWOOD DIED, THERE WERE DAYS OF HEAVY RAIN. HER **CASKET** FLOATED TO THE SURFACE."

GRACE IS BACK!

"EVEN TODAY, PEOPLE CLAIM TO SEE A GHOSTLY WOMAN WALKING ALONG THE OCEAN SHORE."

"SOME BELIEVED THAT SHERWOOD'S SPIRIT ROSE DURING THE FULL MOON AND HOWLED IN A TREE NEAR HER GRAVE."

NAMES SUCH AS WITCHDUCK ROAD, WITCHDUCK POINT, AND SHERWOOD LANE NEAR VIRGINIA BEACH REMIND US OF SHERWOOD'S STORY.

IN 2006, SHERWOOD WAS PARDONED BY THE GOVERNOR OF VIRGINIA. THEY EVEN PUT UP A STATUE IN HER HONOR!

WAS SHE REALLY A WITCH?

WELL, PROBABLY NOT.

"YET IN THE MORNING FOG OR IN THE QUIET NIGHT, FEW WILL WALK NEAR WITCHDUCK POINT WITHOUT THINKING OF THE WITCH OF PUNGO."

More Witch Stories

- Goodwife Joan Wright was the first person accused of witchcraft in Virginia. The case occurred in 1626 near Jamestown. A number of witnesses spoke at her trial. Giles Allington said that when he did not hire Joan Wright as a **midwife** she became angry. She cast a spell on his wife and child that made them sick. The child died shortly after it was born. Other witnesses said that Wright correctly predicted when certain members of the town would die, proving she was a witch.

- In Virginia in 1698, John and Anne Byrd sued two of their neighbors for making false statements against Anne. They said Charles Kinsey and John Potts accused Anne of riding them like a broomstick at night up and down the seashore. They said that she was a witch and had made a pact with the Devil. One of the men finally admitted that he might have just dreamed that it happened.

- A story comes from early Virginia history about a witch who fell in love with a man on a neighboring farm. To be near him, she changed herself into a deer and went to his farm. The man, wanting the deer for food, shot at it and hit it in the foot. The deer ran away. Later the man noticed that the woman who lived next door had lost her hand.

Glossary

accused (uh-KYOOZD) Said someone did something bad.

attacked (uh-TAKD) Tried to hurt someone or something.

bewitched (bih-WICHD) Cast a spell on someone or something.

casket (KAS-ket) A long box that holds a dead person who is to be buried.

convict (kun-VIKT) To find or prove someone guilty.

innocence (IH-nuh-sens) Having done nothing wrong.

jury (JOOR-ee) A group of people chosen to make a decision in a court case based on the facts given to them.

magistrates (MA-jih-strayts) People in charge of the courts.

midwife (MID-wyf) A person who helps women during childbirth.

pacts (PAKTS) Agreements.

pardoned (PAR-dun-ed) Excused someone who may have done something wrong.

predicted (prih-DIKT-ed) Made a guess based on facts or knowledge.

sued (SOOD) Sought justice from a person by taking legal action.

victim (VIK-tim) A person or an animal that is harmed or killed.

Index

Web Sites

Due to the changing nature of Internet links, PowerKids Press has developed an online list of Web sites related to the subject of this book. This site is updated regularly. Please use this link to access the list:

www.powerkidslinks.com/mons/witches/